Seeds of Faith

I Feel

Karissa Jekel / Subi

I feel the world around me
and dream of where I'd like to go.
I feel my body listening.
I want to learn about so many things!

I feel the world around me
in lands of ice and snow.
Smooth and shiny penguins live in Antarctica,
and furry polar bears in the northern Arctic.

I feel the world around me
from sun-up to sundown.
Tropical Hawaiian breezes tickle my skin
and the ocean's waves sing me a lullaby.

I feel the world around me
as the hot Egyptian sun pours down.
I feel small gazing at the pyramids,
but exploring will be fun!

I feel the world around me
as the rainforest canopy touches the sky.
I feel like part of the Amazon,
with its amazing animals and birds.

I feel the world around me
in Australia, down under.
I see koalas, kangaroos and kookaburras
from a tall eucalyptus tree.

I feel the world around me
in an ancient bamboo forest in China.
The mist kisses my face
as the pandas munch on bamboo plants.

I feel the world around me
on the plains of Africa's
Kalahari Desert.

I feel the playful nudge of a meerkat
asking me to help him dig tunnels in the dirt.

I feel the world around me
as I sit by the sea in Spain.
The waves crash upon the rocks,
spraying my toes with water.

I feel the world around me
as the northern lights flicker

in the Arctic sky.
I stand in wonder at this heavenly sight!

I feel the world inside me.
I feel it deep in my heart.
Here at home, light and love surround me
and my spirit soars!

I feel the world inside me
as I send my love around the globe.
I feel grateful when I think of our
beautiful world and I feel happy
knowing that God loves all creation.

I feel the world inside me
and I know God has a special plan for me.
I can feel God with me in my heart
everywhere I go!

Activity

Take a Whisper Walk Together

On a warm summer evening or a brisk autumn afternoon, take a whisper walk with your child. The rules are simple: no talking while you walk. (If you must talk a little, you may whisper.) Spend about 20 or 30 minutes on the walk.

Look around. What do you see? What do you hear and smell? What is the weather like? How do you feel when you experience these things: happy, sad, excited, worried, peaceful? Do you feel God's presence? The point of this activity is to begin to recognize and identify your true inner feelings in this moment. Be aware of these as you walk and quietly enjoy each other's company.

You may be surprised to see things you've never noticed before. It's hard at first not to speak, but you will likely find that the silence allows your minds and hearts to wander freely. When you get home, take time to share these feelings with each other.

Prayer

Dear God,

You are the Creator of the universe.
Help me to see and feel you
in everything and everyone around me,
and to share your love with others.
Amen.

I am always aware of the
Lord's presence; he is near.
Psalm 16:8

Originally published by Gemser Publications, Spain
Layout: Gemser Publications, S.L.
© Gemser Publications, S.L. 2011
El Castell, 38 08329 Teià (Barcelona, Spain)
www.mercedesros.com

Novalis Publishing Office
10 Lower Spadina Avenue, Suite 400
Toronto, Ontario, Canada
M5V 2Z2

This edition © 2012 Novalis Publishing Inc.
Cover design: Audrey Wells
Adaptation of text: Anne Louise Mahoney
Published by Novalis
www.novalis.ca

Head Office
4475 Frontenac Street
Montréal, Québec, Canada
H2H 2S2

Library and Archives Canada Cataloguing in Publication
        Jekel, Karissa
        I feel / Karissa Jekel ; Subi, illustrator.

        (Seeds of faith)
        ISBN 978-2-89646-475-3

        1. Emotions--Juvenile literature. 2. Emotions--Religious aspects--Christianity--Juvenile
        literature. I. Subirana, Joan II. Title. III. Series: Jekel, Karissa. Seeds of faith.

        BV4597.3.J45 2012   j248.4   C2012-901219-X

Printed in China.

We acknowledge the financial support of the Government of Canada through the Canada Book
Fund for business development activities.

5   4   3   2   16   15